History, Guilt, and Habit

OTHER BOOKS BY OWEN BARFIELD

Published by Wesleyan University Press

What Coleridge Thought

Speaker's Meaning

Romanticism Comes of Age
(new and augmented edition)

Unancestral Voice

Worlds Apart: A Dialogue of the 1960's

Poetic Diction: A Study in Meaning
(third edition, with afterword by the author)

The Rediscovery of Meaning, and Other Essays

Published Elsewhere

History in English Words

Saving the Appearances: A Study in Idolatry

OWEN BARFIELD

History,
Guilt, and Habit

WESLEYAN UNIVERSITY PRESS

Middletown, Connecticut

Copyright © 1979 by Owen Barfield

Library of Congress Cataloging in Publication Data

Barfield, Owen, 1898–
History, guilt, and habit.

I. Title.
AC8.B4247   081   79–65333
ISBN 0–8195–5038–8

Distributed by Columbia University Press
136 South Broadway, Irvington, N.Y. 10533

Manufactured in the United States of America
First edition

History is the 'Know Thyself' of humanity,
the self-consciousness of mankind.

J. G. Droysen

Contents

Foreword

BY G. B. TENNYSON

IN HIS autobiography C. S. Lewis wrote of Owen Barfield that he was the type of every man's "Second Friend . . . the man who disagrees with you about everything. He is not so much the *alter ego* as the antiself." Although Lewis was speaking of Barfield's relation to Lewis himself, something of the same sort can be said about Barfield's relation to modern thought generally. Even the term "antiself," with its Yeatsian mystical overtones, seems just the right one for a mind that engages so much of contemporary thought and yet does so from a wholly different and in many ways uncontemporary perspective. Lewis went on to describe how the Barfieldian antiself worked in relation to his own thought, and this passage too, *mutatis mutandis*, il-

Owen Barfield

luminates something of the special quality of Barfield's mind in relation to his readers:

> Of course he shares your interests; otherwise he would not become your friend at all. But he has approached them all at a different angle. He has read all the right books but has got the wrong thing out of every one. It is as if he spoke your language but mispronounced it. How can he be so nearly right and yet, invariably, just not right? . . . When you set out to correct his heresies, you find that he forsooth has decided to correct yours!

Just as with "antiself," Lewis' diction in this passage is wonderfully telling for the quality of Barfield's thought, and his account of their intellectual opposition adapts itself to the wider theme of Barfield and the modern world. Barfield shares many of the interests of that world — from anthropology to myth to psychology to semantics — and yet he has "approached them all at a different angle." He has read not only the right books but it often seems all possible books; yet from a modern view he has taken the wrong things from them. He speaks the language of the modern world

Foreword

— indeed, one of his multiple intellectual lifetimes has been devoted to the study of words and language, and he is a master of a clear and supple contemporary English prose — but from the modern point of view he is somehow mispronouncing it. Sometimes he seems to be speaking an earlier form of English, late medieval perhaps, at other times a future English not yet fully grasped by any other contemporary speaker. As for heresies, how else refer to Barfield's deep concern with philosophy, theology, religion, and at the same time his insistent perception of value in these very activities long viewed as outmoded by clever moderns? The only aspect of the passage that cannot be transferred to Barfield and the modern world is any implication that Lewis himself would stand anywhere but on Barfield's side. For Lewis' quarrel with Barfield was an intellectual family quarrel, even if it was referred to grandly as the Great War. And, as Lewis acknowledged, "I think he changed me a good deal more than I him."

If any book by Owen Barfield is likely to change the thinking of the public as Barfield changed the thinking of C. S. Lewis, it is the

Owen Barfield

present volume. Here are three succinct lectures containing in them Barfield's leading ideas for the past half-century and more, expressed in such a way as to make those ideas accessible to any intelligent and fair-minded reader. The lectures treat the past, the present, and the future as these have been the subjects of Barfield's lifetime concern. The knowing Barfieldian will find here reflections of Barfield's whole corpus and will want to turn back again to some of his stimulating earlier works. And I venture to say that the reader coming upon Barfield for the first time in this compact presentation will sense the resonance of the wisdom of a lifetime and be led to a similar pursuit. A glance at these lectures in the light of Barfield's previous work may help to show why such a pursuit is worthwhile, why it is that Barfield's concerns should concern us all.

There is scarcely a single term that comprehends the range of Owen Barfield's interests and learning, though "philosopher" would probably do as well as any, but all of his interests have been grounded in his study of history,

Foreword

which is to say something more than that he is a student of history. He is rather a knower of history and a thinker about it. *History* is not only the first word of the title of this volume and of the first lecture, it is the subject of Barfield's earliest writings. Thus "History of Ideas: Evolution of Consciousness" takes us back to Barfield's first full-length work of nonfiction, *History in English Words* (1926), and with it back to the peculiarly Barfieldian insight amounting to a discovery that the history of language contains within it a record of the evolution of human consciousness. Here was Barfield coming at things from another angle. In so doing he single-handedly redeemed the study of etymology and created a new field for investigation. His understanding of the evolution of consciousness, coupled with his fruitful distinction grounded in Romantic and Coleridgean philosophy between perception and thinking, formed the framework for his dazzling examination of the language of poetry, *Poetic Diction* (1928). These two are the key works behind Barfield's first lecture, though other and later works play their part as well. What is especially new and

Owen Barfield

useful in the current presentation is Barfield's distinction between the evolution of consciousness and the history of ideas with which it is always in danger of being confused or conflated. Both are worthy studies, but the academic world has concentrated almost exclusively on the latter and often in too arid a way. Barfield shows the enormous potential for understanding the past, including the history of ideas, by appreciating the evolution of consciousness.

"Modern Idolatry: The Sin of Literalness" is an application of Barfield's understanding of the evolution of consciousness to the modern world, to our present discontents as the products of that idolatry he confronted so luminously in *Saving the Appearances* (1957). It incorporates as well the wisdom that Barfield has distilled from a lifetime of reflection on Romanticism and the Romantics. Here Barfield has certainly been reading the right books, as his essays collected in *Romanticism Comes of Age* (1944, rev. 1967) have already shown, and as his more recent, deeply pondered *What Coleridge Thought* (1971) and the essays in *The Rediscovery of Meaning* (1977)

Foreword

proved anew. What is more, he *has* been getting the right things from his reading. He has in fact salvaged for serious contemporary consideration such Coleridgean ideas (to take as example his chief source of inspiration from among the Romantics) as that of polarity, interpenetration, and reconciliation of opposites. It is fitting that the 1976 *Festschrift* in Barfield's honor should have borne the title *Evolution of Consciousness* and the subtitle *Studies in Polarity*.

Barfield's understanding of the evolution of consciousness and his application of the concept of polarity have enabled him to see that the modern perception of the world is dangerously one-sided, that this one-sidedness is at bottom the chief cause of modern alienation. By making plain that idolatry is not a mere fanciful use of a theological concept but the actual state of received modern consciousness, Barfield is also able to explicate the connection between sin and madness and to illuminate the pervasive modern problem of guilt. There is no doubt here that the author of *Speaker's Meaning* (1967) is pronouncing the language correctly.

Owen Barfield

The third lecture in the series, "The Force of Habit," is probably the most invigorating of all, for it is the one in which Barfield undertakes to look toward the future and to tell us what should be done. Out of the study of history and the light it sheds on modern idolatry comes Barfield's awareness of the force, nay, the tyranny of habit that prompts the question: what do we do in the face of the imbalance in our received thinking-perceiving? Barfield answers this question in a typically tactful and understated way. What he calls for is a revolution, or, perhaps better said, a reformation. But it is the best kind, the sort that Carlyle called "the only solid" kind of reformation, one that "each begins and perfects on *himself.*" Interestingly, Carlyle spoke of that kind of reformation in writing of the "Signs of the Times," which is what Barfield has been reading with such uncanny accuracy and about which he is more than "nearly right."

The future that Barfield gently warns us is looming if we do not begin to perform individually that silent but solid reformation is a future that C. S. Lewis also became concerned about in *The Abolition of Man.* Just as Barfield

Foreword

is Lewis' antiself, he comes at the problem of
the future from another, subtler angle; but it is
an angle that leads to an understanding very
like Lewis' own, and a prescription that is
wholly Barfield's. Readers of Barfield will hear
in his words here echoes and reverberations of
almost all of his works, even including those
haunting, lesser-known pieces like *This Ever
Diverse Pair* (1950), *Worlds Apart* (1963), and
Unancestral Voice (1965), to say nothing of
his abundant and too little known anthro-
posophical writings of six decades. Barfield has
forsooth set about to correct some modern
heresies, the greatest of these being our insistent refusal to look at what he calls the "inside"
of things and to take instead the outside as the
only reality and to fall down and worship it.
Like the kindly prophet he is, Barfield does not
denounce this generation of vipers: he seeks
rather to open the eyes of the blind and to
unstop the ears of the deaf. This is the en-
deavor of a charitable as well as a wise man.

In *History, Guilt, and Habit* Owen Barfield
expresses the hope that, while each lecture
should stand on its own (for they were deliv-

ered to somewhat different audiences), the whole is designed to constitute a "tri-unity." I think readers will recognize such a tri-unity in this work and that they will find it as well in all of Barfield's writings. It is a tri-unity that has about it something of the quality of that better-known theological tri-unity, though here the appropriate terms would be something like Past, Present, and Future held distinct in time but one in eternity in a unity of meaning. For it is meaning that Barfield gives back to us in the face of all the contemporary assertions that meaning has fled forever, was indeed never there but as a projection of those also meaningless nerve ganglia we call minds. *Poetic Diction* bore the pregnant subtitle *A Study in Meaning,* and the true meaning of meaning has never been far from Barfield's thought. That is the wisdom he brings us from the past.

That meaning itself is in danger of being discarded is what his wisdom teaches us about the present. Here again the subtitle of another masterful work, *Saving the Appearances,* points the lesson — *A Study in Idolatry.* Thus Barfield has been more than a recoverer; he has

Foreword

been, as Arnold said of Goethe, "physician to the iron age."

But as one whose thought has been so fruitfully energized by that of Rudolf Steiner, Barfield has not been content to stop with the rediscovery of the past and the diagnosis of the present. He has always looked to the future. The final and highest aim of all his endeavors is to point to how we can maintain and enrich that meaning once so immediate, now so fugitive. The key lies in the concept Steiner found central in Goethe and Barfield central in Coleridge — the active and participating Imagination. Through it Barfield believes that Romanticism will truly come of age.

The role of the imagination in Barfield's own work is what most sets him apart from the run of philosophers and makes him a poet as well. It is C. S. Lewis again who tells the story of having once spoken in Barfield's presence of philosophy as a "subject." Barfield observed, "It wasn't a *subject* to Plato; it was a way." But for philosophy to become again a way — "a way back and a way forward," as Barfield remarked in another context — one must exercise the imagination as Barfield has

Owen Barfield

done. To do so, even in some small degree, is
to begin to realize, among many other things,
that Barfield is not so much our antiself as our
better self.

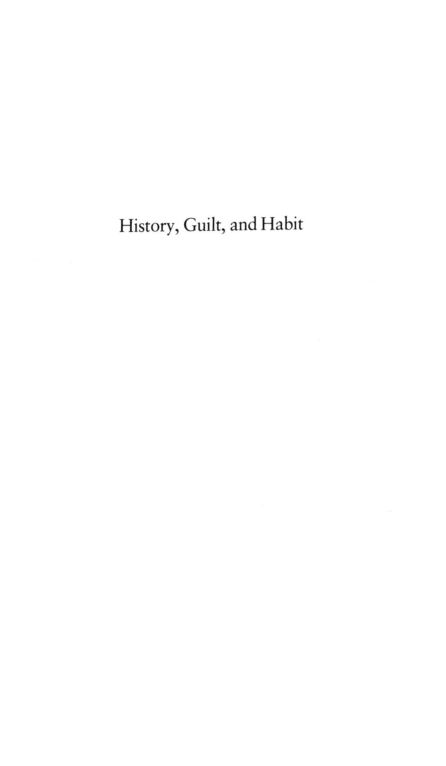

History, Guilt, and Habit

I

History of Ideas:
Evolution of Consciousness

IS THERE ANY real difference between what we mean when we use the word "evolution" and what we mean when we use the word "history"? It sometimes looks as if there is not. Whether you talk about the history of the earth or the evolution of the earth, or of mankind, makes no difference. On the other hand, the terms are not *always* interchangeable. No biologist would talk about the history of species, and no historian would refer to the evolution of the Peloponnesian War. This shows, I think, that there really are two different concepts involved, and that we should do well to keep them distinct in our minds, whether or not we allow them to overlap in the looseness of casual speech.

What then is the difference? It seems to me

Owen Barfield

that the historian R. G. Collingwood was laying his finger on it when he argued in *The Idea of History*[1] that "all history is history of thought." Maybe, by putting it in just that way, he was spoiling a good case by overstating it; but whether that is so or not, he was drawing attention, and drawing it usefully, to the fact that, when we speak of history, we have in mind, or ought to have in mind, something that imports a consciously directed process. At least in some degree a conscious process. There may be, even in recent history (as Marxism for instance maintains), much in the process that is going on unconsciously, but in order to be historical, it must be in some measure a conscious process.

And that surely is what distinguishes it from evolution. By contrast with history, evolution is an unconscious process. Another, and perhaps a better, way of putting it would be to say that evolution is a natural process, history a human one; since nature, in its higher development, does of course include animal consciousness. I do not however think we can

1. Oxford: Clarendon Press, 1946; Oxford: Oxford University Press (Oxford Paperbacks), 1961.

say it includes *human* consciousness — not, that is, unless we are happy to smudge our vocabulary. Nature, someone will say, includes human nature. Very well, but insofar as we treat man as a part of nature — for instance in a biological survey of evolution — we are precisely *not* treating him as a historical being. As a historically developing being, he is set over against nature, both as a knower and as a doer, and we can no longer consider him simply as a part of nature — unless of course when we say "nature," we really mean "everything"; in which case the word ceases to be of much use to anyone. One of the disadvantages of being an out-and-out materialist is that you can no longer use the word "nature" with any consistency, because in your system it includes everything; just as one of the disadvantages of being an out-and-out idealist is that you can no longer use the word "spirit" meaningfully, because in your system it includes everything.

When Collingwood contrasted the *study* of history with the *science* of nature as sharply as he did, he was concerned primarily with historical *events*. Historical events (he gave as an example Caesar crossing the Rubicon) are dif-

5

ferent from natural events, inasmuch as they are always in some measure the result of, or accompanied by, *thoughts*. He went on to say that we only really experience history, and therefore we only study it properly, to the extent that we "re-enact" in our own minds the thoughts which preceded and accompanied the actions it records. As a theory of history in general this latter contention has been disputed, by historians and others; but that need not concern us now, because, whether or not it is true of history as a whole, it is certainly true of one branch of history. Whether or not it is true of the history of man as doer, it is self-evidently true of the history of man as knower — or, if you like, as would-be knower. You cannot study the history of thought without thinking the thoughts whose history you are studying.

This particular branch of history, which I am calling the history of man as knower, has been attracting increasing attention in the last few decades under the title history of ideas. What sort of discipline then do people usually have in mind when they speak of history of ideas, and perhaps create an academic department with that label on it? Maybe something like this: instead of wrestling, head on, with — let us say — the philosophy of Aristotle, and asking where he was right and where he was wrong, we trace how the ideas that constitute that philosophy arose as corrections, modifications, refutations of the philosophies of Plato and the pre-Socratics before him; and then we observe how those ideas were themselves corrected, modified, refuted by later thinkers; we arrive by that route at the Scholastic philosophers of the Middle Ages, and by the like dialectical progression on to Francis Bacon, Descartes, the English Empiricists, Kant and so forth.

Such a discipline is undoubtedly a very valuable one, provided it is conscientiously and not superficially pursued. But it is based on a certain assumption, which it is my principal purpose to question. It assumes that all these philosophers were asking themselves the same questions and then finding different answers to them; that they were talking about the same things, and merely reasoning differently about

them. That means that the history of philosophy is treated, in effect, as though it were a
dialogue between contemporaries.[2]

Of course history of ideas is not confined to
the history of philosophy; but I think you will
find this same assumption underlying the history of ideas, as it is commonly approached
and treated, in other domains as well, whether
it be ideas in religion or politics or science. To
explain why I question that assumption, I
must go back to the difference — and, arising
out of that, the relation — between history
and evolution. I have called one of them a natural process and the other a human process;
and it follows from that that there is, to begin
with, a simple chronological relation between
the two. History is *later* than evolution. It only
came into being after evolution had already
had a long innings. The physical basis on
which our thinking rests had to acquire something like its present form before there could

2. A very unfair dialogue, since in the nature of
things the predeceasing disputant had no right of reply.
The point is that the ideas are taken as related in the
mode of dialogue. The thread on which they are strung
is a dialectical one only.

History of Ideas

be a dawning of what we call "ideas." Let me leave aside for the moment the question whether it is also a mutually exclusive relation; whether, that is, history must also be thought of as progressively *replacing* evolution, or whether the two processes can continue side by side. For, whatever we may think about that, the chronological relation raises another question which I would rather consider first. When — at what stage in the process of evolution — did thought first make its appearance, and history in its proper sense therefore begin?

Obviously we are taken back by such reflections into a long period which is sometimes loosely designated "prehistory"; a period when man, both as doer and as knower, must have been already active, although we have no surviving records of him. It is a period about which there has been any amount of speculation, and plenty of unsupported assumptions. There is however one assumption which I think *must* be made: that there is something else which made its appearance on the stage of evolution before thought could do so, and that is *perception*. I hope you will allow me to use that term rather loosely —

more loosely than it could be used, for instance, in any epistemological theory of perception. I mean it to cover a wide gamut, ranging from what is better called "sensation" at one end of the scale to what is better called "feeling" at the other end. Because I want only to fix attention on that point in nature — whether we are speaking diachronically of evolution, or synchronically of the ascending scale of organisms in the present — or again, of individual mental development up to the beginning of self-consciousness — on that point at which nature becomes a duality: the point at which there is both an outer and an inner to be considered. Call it the point at which *consciousness* appears, if you like; but I have to eschew that term for the moment, because consciousness, *for us,* normally includes thinking; and the distinction between thinking and perceiving is just what I have now to emphasize.

It is one of those distinctions which is obvious, without being sharp or clear. It is obvious, and remains obvious, to every normal mind, although when we come to to analyze it, we may not be able to rule a boundary line. It remains obvious, as the distinction between day and night remains obvious, though, when we begin to analyze that distinction, we come up against such refinements as dusk and twilight. There is more than one way of characterizing the difference. Perception is essentially a passive experience, something that *happens* to us; thinking is an active one, something that we *do*. Or if you don't like this distinction, because of refinements such as the "intentionality" which some have detected (rightly, I would say) in perception, or on the other hand because of the passivity of that uncontrolled type of thinking called "reverie," then thoughts are something that comes from within; perceptions something that comes from without. The point is not how we choose to characterize it, but that we all realize the distinction as a matter of course and without any real difficulty.

Unless, of course, we go out of our way to lose sight of it, as some philosophers who ought to have known better have done. One of the most valuable lessons I learned from Coleridge was to detect that terribly obsessive, and terribly contemporary, fallacy which supposes that we must only *distinguish* things that we are also able to *divide.* It is closely allied to an obsession with space as the criterion of reality. When we divide things, we set them, either in fact or in imagination, side by side in space. But space is not the be-all and end-all, and there are many things that, by reason of their interpenetration — I repeat, because of their *interpenetration* — cannot be divided, though they are easily distinguished: acquaintance and friendship, for example, or envy and hatred. We shall see, I hope, that for human consciousness as it is today, thinking and perceiving come within that class.

Let me pause for a moment, before proceeding, upon this obsessive confusion between distinguishing and dividing. I call it an obsession because I see it as one of those ingrained habits of thought, of which it is difficult to say whether they are conscious or unconscious. It is that mental habit (and this also is something which Coleridge perceived so clearly) that has been both cause and effect of the whole direction taken by natural science since the Scientific Revolution; I mean the concentration of attention always on smaller and smaller units — molecules, atoms, neurons, genes, hormones, etc. — as the only direction in which advancing knowledge can proceed. The beneficial results of such a combination of reduction and concentration, for the purposes of technology and manipulation, need no stressing. But again, like space itself, technology and manipulation are not the be-all and end-all, not, at all events, for me. In any case their usefulness for the study of such matters as history and evolution is, to say the least of it, marginal. And my subject *is* evolution and history. I will only add, before returning to it, that, however impressive may be the practical justification for this atomic obsession, there is no evidential justification whatever for the conclusion, or rather the assumption, to which it so often leads, namely, that the parts preceded the wholes, and that the world was actually built by putting together the units into which our minds divide it, as a house is built by putting bricks together.

Interesting attempts have been made to arrive at the relation between thinking and perceiving by imagining them actually divided from each other. You may remember William

Owen Barfield

James's supposition of a confrontation between, on the one hand, the environment — all that we usually mean by the word "nature" — and, on the other, a man who possessed all the organs of perception, but who had never done any thinking. He demonstrated that such a man would perceive nothing, or nothing but what James called "a blooming, buzzing confusion." Well, he was only expressing in his own blunt way the conclusion which always is arrived at by all who make the same attempt, whether philosophers, psychologists, neurologists, or physicists. Unfortunately it is also a conclusion which is commonly *forgotten* by the same philosophers, psychologists, neurologists, and physicists almost as soon as it has been arrived at; or certainly as soon as they turn their minds to other matters — such as history or evolution — but which I personally decline to forget. I mean the conclusion, the irrefragable consensus, that what we perceive is structurally inseparable from what we think.

In particular I decline to forget it when I try to fix my attention on such matters as evolution and history, and the relation be-

tween them. I refuse to forget, when I am in
that room in the library, what all those
philosophers and neurologists and so forth
taught me in the other rooms, namely, that
what we perceive is structurally inseparable
from what we think. With what result? Here I
must come, for a time, the nearest I hope I
shall need to come to what is commonly dis-
paraged under the name of "metaphysics."
You will sometimes hear people say they have
no metaphysics. Well, they are lying. Their
metaphysics are implicit in what they take for
granted about the world. Only they prefer to
call it "common sense." And at this point in
my lecture unfortunately I have to question
rather radically what, under the present dispensation, the great majority of people do take
for granted about the world. This involves putting the question: what do we really mean
when we use the expression "what we perceive"? and putting it without, at the same
time, conveniently forgetting that what we
perceive is structurally inseparable from what
we think. And the answer is that we can only
mean the very world itself. Or at all events the
macroscopic world itself. The physicists, as

Owen Barfield

you know, have been telling us for a long time that, in addition to that, or somehow underlying it, there is the microscopic and submicroscopic world; moreover that it is only this microscopic and submicroscopic world that exists independently of ourselves; only that world that has an objective existence. Some philosophers[3] have added that it is therefore only knowledge of *that* world that can really be called knowledge at all.

Evolutionists and historians must think differently. The knowledge they are aiming at *is* knowledge of the macroscopic world. And that — as I have been emphasizing — *is* unquestionably both subjective and objective. When a historian, for instance, talks about Caesar crossing the Rubicon, or any man crossing any river, he does not mean by the word "river" simply a combination of oxygen and hydrogen; he means a rich assemblage of qualities like coldness, gurgling, flashing in the sun. When he is describing Napoleon's retreat from Moscow, the word "cold" does not

3. Notably the group, including Bertrand Russell and G. E. Moore, who came to be known as "the Cambridge Realists."

signify a thermometer reading; it means the felt quality "cold." And when an evolutionist refers to redwoods or red deer, he is not referring to vibrations or light waves, but the quality "red." All quality is subjective as well as objective, and the macroscopic world is compounded of qualities, as well as quantities. It *is* therefore what we perceive and, accordingly, is inseparable from what we think. I hope my vocabulary is not irritating anyone. It doesn't matter what you call it; whether you say "macroscopic" or "real appearance," or whether you borrow from phenomenology and speak of "the world as experienced" or the *monde vécu* — as long as you remember that what we perceive is the actual world, and not a kind of shadow-show pretending to be the actual world (with, of course, an actual world, consisting of particles, mathematical equations or something of the sort, hiding behind it).

Maybe that sounds obvious enough; and if anyone feels that I have merely been laboring the obvious at inordinate length, I can only refer him to George Orwell's observation that "we have now sunk to a depth at which the re-statement of the obvious is the first duty of intelligent men." Obvious as it is, we have to exert a real effort to remember it when we go on to realize a certain consequence it entails. It entails, in particular, that when we speak, as I did a little earlier, about *consciousness,* about the point at which consciousness arose and so forth, we are speaking not merely about human nature, as we call it, but also about nature itself. When we study consciousness historically, contrasting perhaps what men perceive and think *now* with what they perceived and thought at some period in the past, when we study long-term *changes* in consciousness, we are studying changes in the world itself, and not simply changes in the human brain. We are not studying some so-called "inner" world, divided off, by a skin or a skull, from a so-called "outer" world; we are trying to study the world itself from its inner aspect. Consciousness is not a tiny bit of the world stuck on to the rest of it. It is the inside of the whole world. Or, if we are using the term in its stricter sense — excluding therefore the subconscious mind — then it is *part* of the inside of the whole world. That is why, although it is not divided from the outer world, it is so very easily *distinguished* from it. For what is easier than to distinguish the outside of something from its inside? It is just because men have come to distinguish so sharply the one from the other, an inner from an outer, that they have gone on (with some help from the philosopher Descartes) to imagine the inner *divided* from the outer.

I say with some help from Descartes. But the help should not be exaggerated. To say that what we perceive is inseparable from what we think is not the same as saying that what we perceive is dependent on any philosophy. What it *is* dependent on is a collectively and historically hardened *habit* of thought, of which we are no longer conscious. Two very different matters — as any convinced idealist who has just stubbed his toe on a stone will tell you — and as Dr. Johnson *failed* to realize when he thought he was refuting Berkeley by kicking one. And it is precisely because of the great difference between these two that there is a difference between history of ideas on the one hand and history or evolution of consciousness on the other. It is these passive habits of thought, not any ideas we are actively

Owen Barfield

entertaining at the moment, that are inseparable from our perceptions; and it is the changes in *these* with which a history of consciousness must deal.

At this point I think I must forestall a possible objection. While I have been emphasizing — not to say reiterating — this fact of the inseparableness of perception from thought, some of you may have long enough memories to recall that, some time before that, I had observed that, in the longer perspective of human evolution as a whole, perception must have *preceded* thought. But if there could ever be one without the other, then they cannot after all be inseparable! Actually I rather hope this objection *has* occurred to you, because it brings up at once a fundamental difficulty of studying consciousness historically at all. The difficulty is this: you cannot study anything without speaking and reading and writing about it. And you cannot speak or read or write without using language, without using the language of today, as your medium. But the language of today is itself the product, the manifestation, of the very thing you are trying to undermine, so to speak, with your historical depiction of the way in which it came into being. You can dig into the earth with a spade in order to get beneath the surface. The spade is itself a product of the earth, but that does not bother you. But if, by some mysterious dispensation, the spade were part of the very patch of earth you were splitting up, you would be rather nonplussed, because you would destroy the instrument by using it. And that is the sort of difficulty you are up against when it is not the earth you are digging into, but consciousness; and when it is not a spade you are digging with, but language. Some people regard the difficulty as insuperable and reject any study of consciousness itself as impossible. Ludwig Wittgenstein for instance insisted that there are some things you can't say anything about, and that foremost among these is — *saying* itself. However quickly you turn around, you can never see the back of your own head. But I do not think it is quite so bad as that, and Wittgenstein, as far as I know, never tried the historical approach.

In fact, however, the historical approach is all-important. When William James experimented with fancying what perceiving

would be like if it were divorced from thinking, he found it reduced to chaos, to that
"blooming buzzing confusion" of his. This, I
am persuaded, was because he was imagining
it happening *today;* and therefore, when he
thought or spoke of perception, he was thinking of perception as it is today. In other words
he was merely demonstrating the impossibility
of separating what *is* now in fact inseparable.
It is otherwise however if we imagine inseparableness, not (as I think he was doing) in
terms of a kind of molecular aggregation and
interspersal, but in terms of interfusion or
interpenetration. That need not mean losing
sight of the distinction. The distinction between thinking and perceiving is, as I have
said, fundamental and self-evident; and we can
only lose sight of it by deliberately averting our
eyes from it, as the philosopher Hume did, for
instance, when he succeeded in persuading
himself that ideas are nothing but faded sense-
impressions.

If we go ahead with the study of the relation between the two — thinking and perceiving — in terms of real interpenetration,
what sort of results do we get? We shall find in

the first place, I think, that it is not a fixed relation but a variable one, variable in terms of the predominance of the one ingredient over the other. The example of this that comes most readily to hand is the difference between poetry and prose; or perhaps (as it is not external literary forms I am thinking of) better say, between the Poetic Principle and the Prosaic. But I will go on saying poetry and prose for short. If we survey the uses that have been made, and are still being made, of language, we can hardly fail to observe that in general in the language of poetry the perceptual element is proportionately higher than in prose; while in prose the intellectual element predominates over the perceptual. Then, if we continue the survey, we shall find — or so I believe, and certainly many others have so found besides myself — the like variable predominance, when we compare language as a whole in its earlier stages with language in its later stages; or the earlier stage of any one language with its later stages. In the early stage the perceptual element is relatively greater; in the later stages the intellectual element. This is not so much in the *use* that is made of words as it is in the meanings of the words themselves. Thus, in our historical survey of consciousness, we find ourselves looking backward down a perspective which reveals more and more of perception and less and less of thought. And if, along *this* path, we allow our fancy to approach the kind of consciousness that would be all perception and no thought, what do we come to? We come to something that is perhaps equally hard to imagine, but is certainly very different from James's blooming, buzzing confusion. What sort of thing then do we come to? Can anything be said about it?

Let me return for a moment to poetry and prose, or let me now say to the language of imagination on the one hand and the language of abstraction and analyis on the other. There is a certain element in the best poetry, which critics of literature have sometimes striven to indicate and theories of imagination have struggled to formulate, namely, that in the language of imagination at its most powerful we are made to feel a kind of *union* between the observer and what he is observing. Charles Lamb, for instance, could speak of a level of writing at which "the imagination seems to resolve itself into the element it contemplates." If this accords with our experience of poetry — and it certainly accords with mine — then it also says something meaningful about that supposititious condition of consciousness, which would be all perception and no thought. In saying it we have found language itself, not a hindrance but a help. That is because it is a good deal easier to see that *language* arises from an interpenetration of thinking and perceiving than it is to see that consciousness itself does. So that to study language historically, taking into account not only its analytical function but also its poetic substance, is a good way of studying the evolution of consciousness. In doing so we are studying that evolution *from within,* and therefore studying consciousness *itself;* not, as the biologists do, studying the evolution of something else altogether and then, on the basis of that study, making all sorts of unwarranted assumptions about the evolution of consciousness. You will be satisfied with that way only if you are blandly convinced that consciousness is a tiny bit of the world stuck on to the rest of it.

Owen Barfield

Of course the difficulty is still there — the difficulty that made me say I was glad of the objection I envisaged. We have had to use the *word* "perception," because it is the only word we have. And we have had to go on using it about a kind of consciousness that must be so different from what *we* now experience as perception, as to be almost unrecognizable. I believe nevertheless that anyone who has taken the trouble to follow me must agree that, though I may of course be mistaken, I have not simply been talking nonsense. The alternative of using a different word altogether also has its disadvantages. What word? And at what point do we give up using "perception" and start using that other word instead? I myself have occasionally used the word "participation" to try and indicate a predominantly perceptual relation between observer and observed, between man and nature, and one which is nearer to unity than to dichotomy.[4]

I fear the amount of time I have expended

4. For example, in *Poetic Diction,* Middletown, Connecticut: Wesleyan University Press, 1973, chapter IX; and in *Saving the Appearances,* New York: Hillary House, 1957, passim.

on this topic may have given the impression that evolution of consciousness means for me simply a lot of speculation about its origin, or its very early stages. Believe me, it is not so. I have been expatiating on the evolution of perception for two reasons. First, because it gave me an opportunity to look at one of the objections that is sometimes raised to the whole project. And secondly because in doing so I had to sketch the broad conceptual framework within which I do feel the study has to be placed if it is to bear any fruit. The study of natural history at any point is going to be pretty useless unless it is pursued within the broad conceptual framework of evolution — not necessarily Darwinian evolution, but evolution in its essential meaning of the process whereby one form emerges from another — so, I feel sure, will the historical study of consciousness be pretty useless unless it is conceived of as within the longer process of evolution by detachment — emergence from identity with the inner workings of nature, through consciousness, to self-consciousness.

This, it may be worthwhile to observe, is

Owen Barfield

the sequence presented in substance in a book published recently, which has made something of a stir in the United States — to judge by the number of people who ask me if I have read it: Julian Jaynes's *The Origin of Consciousness in the Breakdown of the Bicameral Mind.*[5] The author, it is true, seeks to fit in what he has to say with a theory of a varying relation between the two halves of the brain. But the book is not really about the brain. It is a valuable and well-documented account of the development of consciousness from the earliest times down to our own; and as such I found that it made no difference to the conviction it carried, whether one accepted, or ignored, or rejected the intrusive bits about the brain. Or no, that is not quite true; because they are incompatible with nearly all the rest it was much *more* coherent, and more convincing, if one ignored them.

Just as a book about biology or natural history, although presupposing evolution, is by no means necessarily *about* evolution, so a book or study about the history of conscious-

5. Boston: Houghton Mifflin, 1976.

ness, although presupposing its evolution, need not necessarily be about it. On the contrary, it may well be concerned with the art, the literature, or the science of some particular period, including, last but not least, our own. The difference between reading such a book and reading the general run of books on the same subject will then be something like the difference between entering a shop that sells cut flowers and selecting one or more bunches (which is a perfectly sensible thing to do, but not the *only* thing one can do) and entering a shop that sells growing plants in pots and selecting one or more of *them*.

Let me try to indicate an example, and one that is especially relevant to the relation between history of ideas and history of consciousness. There is no time left in this lecture to do more than indicate. Referring to the history of *ideas*, I spoke near my beginning of its application to philosophy. In that domain history of consciousness must do something more than the sort of things I described. It must take into account the fact that philosophers have, and always have had, to begin from the world they live in — from what they perceive. And it will try to become aware of some of the habit of thought that is structurally inseparable from that world. As one single instance of this: when it has to consider references to the four elements, Fire, Air, Water and Earth in Aristotle's *De Coelo* or his work *Generation and Corruption* or elsewhere, it will not be content to treat these terms as having nearly the same meaning that the corresponding words have in our own language today. It will be very much aware that the perception of these elements common to Aristotle and his contemporaries was much less a perception of something detached from themselves, much more a perception of qualities and processes to be found within themselves, within their own consciousness, as well as without in nature. *They* did not need lectures to remind them that qualities are both objective and subjective. The historian of consciousness will be even more aware of this when he comes on the same terms in the writings of earlier philosophers, Heraclitus for example.

From a background such as this the historian of consciousness may profitably go on to other and wider issues. He may for instance try to review and assess the essential difference between the two primary periods into which he will be inclined to divide any history of man as knower: I mean the period before the birth of philosophy and the period after it. For he will know that philosophy, and later on science, have always performed a dual role. They have operated both as effect and as cause: as effect, inasmuch as they start from and are limited by a mode of perception common at the time of their origin; as cause, inasmuch as, in the further course of time, they themselves help to bring about the formation and fixation of habits of thought divergent from those that prevailed before them. And it is from these divergent habits, from this different perception as their base, that subsequent philosophers will be starting in their turn. The philosophy of Immanuel Kant is based on a Galilean earth and a Copernican universe. He could never have produced it if he had been born a few centuries earlier in a Ptolemaic universe and on an Aristotelian earth.

This leads back to a question I raised nearer the beginning of this lecture, but without then pursuing it. There is no doubt that history, as I have defined it, came *later* than evolution. Are we also to assume that it has *replaced* evolution? Was, for instance, the change from a Ptolemaic into a Copernican world brought about solely by the Scientific Revolution? Many people think so. But I am sure they are oversimplifying a much more complex process. Changes in perception (evolution-of-consciousness changes) are indeed brought about over a long period by changed ideas (history-of-ideas changes). But ideas themselves had begun changing long before the Scientific Revolution: for example, when Nominalism gained the ascendancy over Realism in Scholastic philosophy.[6] Nevertheless not all the changing had been of that kind. Professor Herbert Butterfield in his *Origins of Modern Science*[7] has no doubt that

6. Realism in Scholastic philosophy is not to be confused with the "realism" of the Cambridge Realists (note 3, above). This is one of the rare instances from historical semantics where a word has not only changed its meaning a great deal but has actually changed into its opposite. "Subjective" is another such instance.

7. London: G. Bell, 1949; New York: Macmillan, 1951.

evolution-of-consciousness changes had been going on as well. Let me conclude by reading a brief passage from that illuminating little book:

> Through changes in the habitual use of words, certain things in the natural philosophy of Aristotle had now acquired a coarsened meaning or were actually misunderstood. It may not be easy to say why such a thing should have happened, but men unconsciously betray the fact that a certain Aristotelian thesis simply has no meaning for them any longer — they just cannot think of the stars and heavenly bodies as things without weight even when the books tell them to do so. Francis Bacon seems unable to say anything except that it is obvious that these heavenly bodies have weight, like any other kind of matter which we meet in our experience. . . .

Again a little later the text continues:

> Between the idea of a stone aspiring to reach its natural place at the centre of the universe — and rushing more fervently as it came nearer home — and the idea of a stone accelerating its descent under the constant force of gravity,

there is an intellectual transition which involves a change in men's feeling for matter.

You can call it a change in men's feeling for
matter, or a change in their "reality principle"
or common sense, or what you will. But if Butterfield is right, the change into our present
world, and out of an older one, has been at
least as much an evolution-of-consciousness
change as a history-of-ideas change. And if the
Scientific Revolution has played a prominent
part, as no doubt it has, in strengthening and
ingraining our present habit of perception, we
shall do well to remember that it is an effect as
well as a cause of that continuing change.

Lastly, you may have noticed that, in spite
of the pointed antithesis in the title of this lecture between *history* of ideas and *evolution* of
consciousness, I have been referring in the
course of it sometimes to the evolution and
sometimes to the history of consciousness.
This was not because I regard them as merely
synonymous, but because I also feel that the
two processes, the one unconscious and the
other deliberate, do continue side by side.
Reflections of that nature can lead into far-

reaching questions. What is the nature of the forces that are determining our evolution in addition to those that we rightly classify as historical? I raise this question now at the very end without attempting even to begin to answer it. I will only add that, in my opinion, the true answer is much more likely to be found by investigating the evolution of consciousness, and its relation to the history both of ideas and of consciousness itself, than in any exclusively biological theory, extrapolated into the past from the natural science of the present, however popular and however deeply ingrained such a theory may have become.

2

Modern Idolatry:
The Sin of Literalness

IN MY LAST LECTURE I spent some time
emphasizing the difficulty of saying anything at all about a kind of consciousness different from our own. It is difficult — some
have said it is impossible — for the simple reason that whatever we succeed in saying must
necessarily be the expression of *our own* consciousness. In my own view it is indeed difficult, but it is not impossible. It is not impossible if there are brought to bear on it three
qualities: patience, a certain sensitivity to
words and their meanings, and some historical
imagination. It requires the kind of sensitivity
that Benjamin Whorf, for example, brought to
bear on it in his essays entitled *Language,*

Modern Idolatry

Thought and Reality[1] and particularly perhaps
in his studies of the Hopi Indians; or it is rendered possible by the historical imagination,
which we find, in addition, in a book like
Thorlief Boman's *Hebrew Thought Compared
with Greek*.[2] Both of these books, which I
mention only as examples, are very much concerned with the topic of *language;* and I have
long felt that a sensitive examination of language is a particularly fruitful way of overcom-
ing the difficulty in question.

The reason for this is that, if it is not simply
a different set of *ideas* but a different kind of
consciousness from our own that we are talking about, or trying to talk about, then it is not
merely different thoughts that we shall be concerned with, but also different *perceptions*.
And the interpenetration of thinking and perceiving, of which all our consciousness consists, happens to be more plainly evident in
language than anywhere else. Need I demon-
strate that? Take the most abstract or immaterial word you can think of, and you will find it

1. Cambridge, Massachusetts: M.I.T. Press, 1956.
2. London: SCM Press Ltd., 1960.

has an element of sense-perception in it. Anatole France once amused himself by reducing a group of such words entirely to their sense-components. He took the sentence: "The soul possesses God in the measure that it participates in the Absolute"; and when he had finished with it, it came out something like: "The breath sits on the shining thing in the bushel of the wholly untied." Conversely, if you take the simplest and most material word — *chair* for instance — it is the element of thought, our mental habit of magically fusing it with all other chairs, present or absent, actual or possible, that turns it from a sound into a *name*. Without that fusion it would not be a word at all. It would be a mere noise — even if the noise had been stimulated by the impression made by some particular chair on our senses.

The question I want to begin by asking is: what sort of lessons about the meanings of words can we learn from the patient exercise of historical imagination? And I mean especially about the meanings of our commonest words. Well, the first thing we find, on examining them, is that most of them do have a long

Modern Idolatry

history behind them; moreover that, in one respect at least, that history is the same for pretty well all of them. It always points us back to a cultural period when there was a much closer interpenetration between thinking and perceiving than is the case with us today (as also, since perceiving is so closely allied with feeling, between thinking and feeling). There is any amount of evidence for this, but I only have time to illustrate with a single example. If you take such a word as "heart," you find that today we use it in two distinct and separate ways. Sometimes we intend by it simply a physical organ residing somewhat on the left side of the body. But at other times — when we speak for instance of a "cold heart," or a "warm heart" — we mean something quite different; something that has little, if indeed any, connection in our minds with the physical organ. In fact we should do equally well, and should be expressing ourselves more precisely, if we had two separate words — using some physiological term, like "cardium" for the physical organ, and reserving the word "heart" for conveying the immaterial meaning intended in such expressions as a cold, or a

Owen Barfield

warm, or a kind heart. We should do better to use two different words, and in many many other cases that is just what we have come to do. In the case of words like "soul" and "spirit," for instance, we have come to reserve them exclusively for the immaterial meaning, and to use some other word, like "wind" or "breath," for the material significance that — as Anatole France had discovered — they once also conveyed.[3]

Well, there is nothing much in that, perhaps you are thinking. You are simply telling us that some words can have a metaphorical, a figurative meaning as well as a literal one. We knew that already. I shall be trying to convince you that, on the contrary, there is a great deal in it. For a number of reasons. The first of which is that *all* — or to be safe, let us say virtually all — the words in our modern vocabulary that now have only an immaterial

3. This is discussed more fully in *Speaker's Meaning,* Middletown, Connecticut: Wesleyan University Press. London: Rudolf Steiner Press, 1970, chapter 2. See also my essay "The Meaning of 'Literal' " in *The Rediscovery of Meaning, and Other Essays,* Middletown, Connecticut: Wesleyan University Press, 1977.

Modern Idolatry

meaning, a reference only to the inner experience we call "consciousness," did at one time have a material one, inasmuch as they — either the words themselves or the elements from other languages of which they are composed — referred to some physical object or event. One quick example of that. We speak of "grasping" an idea, and we have only to reflect for a moment to realize that the literal meaning of "grasp" is a physical act. Suppose then we use some other word instead and speak of "conceiving" an idea. We still find, on examination, that the Latin elements of which it is composed referred at one time to the physical kind of grasping. And then, if we care to go further, we are confronted with the fact that all our inward or immaterial meanings can be traced back in the same way to material ones — no matter how remote from it they now seem; and no matter how much *more* remote we try to make them by adding all manner of -isms and -ologies and -ologicals and -ologicalisms, and so forth.

This also will be something of which many of you are no doubt well aware. What I want to draw attention to is the fact that it is a matter which only began to receive the close attention of scholars and others round about the middle of the nineteenth century. I am moreover firmly persuaded that in the thoughts they formed and the things they wrote about it at that time they were all, almost without exception, guilty of two sins: a sin of commission and a sin of omission. The sin of commission lay in this: that, having discovered how so many, if not all, immaterial words formerly had a material reference, they proceeded to assume (though it certainly does not follow) that, *to begin with,* those same words had *only* a material reference, or, if you like, only a "literal" meaning. Whatever "conceiving" signifies today, it originally signified simply and solely "grasping," whether with a man's hand or a monkey's paw. The sin of omission lay in this: that, having observed so clearly how modern words that appear to us to have an exclusively immaterial reference once had a material reference, they *failed* to observe that the converse is also true. They failed to observe that modern words that appear to us to have an exclusively material reference, once also had an immaterial one. It is in fact only at

Modern Idolatry

a very late stage in language that words like "heart" or "sun" (I have to cut down heavily on examples) come to possess, for what we call common sense, their so-called "literal" meanings of a physical organ and a ball of gas.

Let us look first at the sin of commission. How did it come about that so many minds fell into it? It was not only positivists like Jeremy Bentham. Deep thinkers like Emerson, and even Shelley, who also touched on the topic, made the same assumption. Literal meanings, that is physical reference, first; and then — just as poets and critics today speak of an "objective correlative" and deliberately choose something from an outside world to express an inner feeling — the immaterial meanings, the figurative ones, were added to them. So they all assumed. So, I think, most people who are interested in the early history, and perhaps in the origin, of language, still assume today. And yet there is no evidence for it whatever. I remember, when I first began to realize this, I made a considerable effort to discover some fairly common word of what Bentham called "the immaterial language," whose meaning *could* be traced as having arisen in that way — that is, by metaphorical extension from the material — and the only one I could feel at all sure of was "emotion." That does seem, as far as one can tell from the *New English Dictionary,* to have been used in a purely physical sense a little before it acquired its subjective one.[4] For all the rest, as far back as they have been traced, they already had the immaterial reference alongside the material one.

How then did the error come about? In this way, I think: you look back into the history of a word you are still using, and the further back you look, the more you find that its figurative meaning was predominant and its exclusively literal meaning had not yet come into being; and *yet* you assume an earlier stage still, when there was *only* the literal meaning. Why? I think the answer is plain enough. It was because the nineteenth century was the age of what I will call for convenience (though it began before Darwin) the age of Darwinian man. It was imbued even more indelibly than our own age with a mental image of primitive

4. But even here there must be some doubt whether its earlier users were not also referring to a spatial "motion" of animal spirits in the physical body.

man as a being with a system of perception exactly like our own and with a mind very much like our own, except that it was not nearly so well stocked. Therefore — so they reasoned, or so they instinctively assumed — language *must* have begun as a series of cries or grunts or howls that somehow very gradually turned into signs indicating the material objects by which Darwinian man perceived himself to be surrounded; and then, still of course very gradually, that system turned itself into the languages of Homer and Shakespeare and the Bible.

A more patient reflection on the nature of figurative language, and then of the figurative element in all language, is desirable for this reason. If you are prepared to take your courage in both hands and forget nearly everything you have ever learned or half-consciously absorbed about Darwinian man,[5] you are presented with quite a different image of the con-

5. This is likely to require a good deal less courage as time goes on and as the contradictions entailed by any theory of evolution based on exclusively physical causes grow more intrusive. See, for example, *Darwin Retried,* by Norman Macbeth (London: Gambit Incorporated,

Owen Barfield

sciousness of primitive man, as it actually must have been. You come instead to a kind of consciousness that was figurative through and through; a kind of consciousness for which it was impossible to perceive *un*figuratively. But what does one mean when one speaks of perceiving figuratively? One means a kind of consciousness which does not, which cannot, perceive the material merely as such; which in perceiving its environment, perceives at the same time an immaterial within or through, or expressed by it. It does not matter for my present purpose whether this is further analyzed, as I attempted to do in my previous lecture, into a different degree of interpenetration between thinking and perceiving. What does matter is that it is the kind of consciousness for which there is no such thing as a merely "outer" world. The outer and material is always,

and Garnstone Press, 1971) and, in Everymans Library, the outspoken Introduction to the English centenary (1967) edition of *The Origin of Species;* also, more generally, my essay "The Coming Trauma of Materialism" in *Rediscovery of Meaning.* See also chapter 3, note 6 below.

Modern Idolatry

and of its own accord, the expression or representation of an inward and immaterial.

Well, why does it matter? Why does it matter to us that our remote ancestors should have had a consciousness so very different from our own? It matters, so I believe, because of the bearing it has on the nature of reality itself. We speak of "common sense," and a man of common sense is perhaps, above all, a man who does not confuse the real with the unreal. Common sense is, in fact, almost identical with what some have called our "reality principle." But common sense also signifies a sensing that is common to all — the way of perceiving that is shared by all the normal members of a community. Common sense has no doubt about the meanings of common words. It is founded on them. It is one with them. And common sense today assumes that it is the outer world that is real and permanent, while the inner experience we call consciousness, or subjectivity, or our own, or our self, is a fleeting unreality to which it somehow gives birth from time to time. It matters a great deal then, if it be the case, for us to realize that the common sense of today is not something that is valid for all time, but something that has evolved from a common sense that was qualitatively different from it.

I have suggested to you that this older type of common sense was one for which the immaterial was perceived as well, in the act of perceiving the material — not something deliberately *added* to it — by the use of poetic metaphor. Its development, then, has consisted in its becoming blind to one half of reality, while retaining the other. It has come to accept and value the outer for its own sake only and not as the manifestation or garb of another and immaterial component. Reality is assumed to consist of *things,* not of images.

There is another place where this process can be observed to occur, but on a smaller scale and over a shorter period. It can happen with those sacred images, which play such an essential part in most religions. They are intended to be perceived, and they begin by being perceived by the faithful, *as* images. That is, as material representations of an immaterial reality. And then, as time goes on, perception

Modern Idolatry

weakens, or it is atrophied, and the material alone is perceived and felt as real. The sacred images have become sacred *things*, and it is the things themselves that are worshiped or propitiated. They have become, in fact, idols. That is why a little book in which I once attempted to sketch, from this point of view, the evolution of our Western consciousness, for which reality consists of a collection of solid objects in space, bears the subtitle "A Study in Idolatry."[6]

Was it a sensational subtitle? You may think the two kinds of idolatry are very different, inasmuch as the solid objects, which constitute our reality principle, are certainly not worshiped — quite the contrary; the things, into which images have turned, are not sacred things. But the difference is not quite so great after all. If the idols are not sacred, the idolatry itself is. The correlative to sacredness is taboo. And if you think it is not taboo today to question that common sense view of reality, or the validity of that mental picture we have of

6. *Saving the Appearances* (1957), New York: Harcourt Brace, 1965.

Owen Barfield

Darwinian man, just try to get a hearing for it in the media.[7]

In the Old Testament idolatry is condemned as a sin, and indeed as *the* besetting sin. It may be thought that, in referring, as my title does, to this modern idolatry of ours as a "sin," I am merely stretching an analogy beyond what it will bear. As against that, it is arguable, and it is in fact being strenuously argued by a good many modern psychologists and psychoanalysts, that the nature (or at all events the typical manifestations) of sin is something which has itself been changing in the course of human evolution.

At this point I propose to make something of a break in my exposition. Will you please forgive me for jumping a gap, if I give you my assurance that I intend later on to recross it in the opposite direction, and this time in the ordinary way, by a bridge. A year or two ago I learned from what should be a reliable source that every year one man in seven and one woman in fourteen consult a doctor about some form of mental disease, and 600,000

7. This is discussed at greater length in *Speaker's Meaning*, chapter 4.

Modern Idolatry

people in Great Britain are referred to psychiatrists.[8] I had guessed of course that something of the sort was going on, but the actual statistics did surprise me; and I believe there is not much doubt that, if similar statistics were produced for North America, they would be more, not less, impressive. Now the characteristic, the *endemic* mental disease of today is some form or other of schizophrenia, which is in effect what used to be called insanity, or madness, and in its extreme development is still so called. There are two things that are noticeable about the modern psychology I have just referred to. The first is that the root, the subconscious root, of schizophrenia is increasingly being traced to the experience of what I will for the moment call "cut-offness." The second is that that experience is increasingly being regarded, not as one that is peculiar to the patient, but in a greater or less degree as one that is the predicament of humanity, or certainly of Western humanity, as a whole. "Everybody without exception must be regarded as

8. Professor Colin Blakemore, in No. 6 of the *Reith Lectures*, 1976 (BBC broadcast, December 1976, and subsequently printed in *The Listener*).

Owen Barfield

schizoid," says, for example, Ronald Fairbairn in his *Object-Relations Theory of the Personality*.[9] If in some cases it reaches the clinical stage, that is merely because the reaction against the cut-offness of humanity as a whole happens here to be more violent than usual. The clinically schizoid are simply the ones who are becoming most sharply aware of it. Thus, they speak of the personality, or the self, as being isolated, encapsulated, excluded, estranged, alienated. There are many different ways of putting it. But what the self of each of us feels isolated *from,* cut off *from,* by its encapsulation in the nakedly physical reality presented to it by the common sense of contemporary culture, is precisely its own existential source. The trouble is, that such an empirical self, founded as it were on its own physical encapsulation, is a false self, *without* reality. It is the kind of self which behaviorist psychology has to mention occasionally, in order to deny its existence. The true Self of everyone remains united — not co-extensive but united — with its original source in the spirit.

9. New York: Basic Books, 1954.

Modern Idolatry

And the mental illness now recognized as schizophrenia comes of the frantic efforts, sometimes aggressive, sometimes defensive, made by the imprisoned personality to fortify and preserve this fictitious self — which is really a nothingness — from destruction. Instead — and that way sanity lies — of taking the hint, as it were, and learning to abandon it in favor of the true Self. The resulting conflicts and the sickness, sometimes amounting to insanity, that those efforts may end in, arise from an invasion of this artificial self by the true, existential self. The personality remains subconsciously aware of its ultimate dependence on this real self for its very existence, while consciously resisting its still, small voice with every cunning device it can invent. The patient's unstable behavior is thus a disguised form of evasive action. He is determined, as R. D. Laing has put it, "to evade becoming himself."

Inevitably, I have been trying to say a very great deal in a very few words. I shall do better to refer you to a recently published book, which includes a brief survey of this psychology of schizophrenia, and to which I am heavily indebted for this part of my lecture. *Sin and Madness,* by Dr. Shirley Sugerman,[10] in addition to surveying much that others have written on the psychopathology of schizophrenia, argues, convincingly to my mind, that what is now conceived and felt as insanity can only be properly understood as the evolutionary metamorphosis of what was formerly conceived and felt as sin. Even in religious circles, or in a good many of them, people today tend to avoid using the word "sin" except by way of metaphor (as when I myself spoke earlier of "sins of omission" and "sins of commission"). Outside of such circles people don't mention sin. They have been liberated from that feeling of guilt for their individual transgressions, which the word "sin" denotes.

But can there be sin without guilt? Paul Ricoeur, in his book *The Symbolism of Evil,*[11] observes, rightly I think, that a feeling of guilt is the fundamental experience of sin. If so,

10. Philadelphia: Westminster Press, 1976. (The author is a practising psychologist in New Jersey and Adjunct Associate Professor at Drew University.)

11. Boston: Beacon Press, 1967 (translated from the French).

Modern Idolatry

how can this contemporary madness, from which there is evidence that we all suffer, but about which we certainly do not feel guilty, have anything to do with sin? Perhaps because, although we do not feel guilty *about* the sin, we do feel guilty *because of* it.

Are people feeling guilty nowadays? Well, if I were asked to lay my finger on one of the most striking differences between the social climate of Europe and the West as it is today and as it was, say sixty years ago, I think I should have to specify the presence in it almost everywhere of a vague, uneasy feeling of guilt. There is an *atmosphere* of guilt. Take for instance the issue of racialism, the relation between the advanced and the so-called "backward nations," or between white and colored. Today people not only want to right the wrongs that have been done in the past, they feel personally guilty about them. It was not so until recently. What was until recently called "the white man's burden" was a burden of responsibility, not a burden of guilt. I am of course speaking psychologically, and not politically; of what was felt and said therefore, as much as what was done. From that point of view, how far the sense of responsibility connoted by such a watchword as "white man's burden" may have been distorted into an excuse for exploitation is irrelevant. Opportunities for self-deception are never far away from any of us. In any case that is not the only instance I could give. People seem almost to go out of their way to find things to feel guilty about, or to encourage others to feel guilty about. The theory of crime and punishment is another instance. In England strange things are said in pulpits and elsewhere, when for instance a young man knocks down an old woman and, not content with robbing her, kicks her about the head just for the fun of the thing before running away. It is not (we are told) the underprivileged young man, but society as a whole that is guilty. Muggings are not to be thought of as crimes, but as "cries for help." Of course there is also some reaction against guilt. The actual phrase "we are *all* guilty!" became such a well-worn cliché that it has nearly died of ridicule. But if the cliché has gone, the climate nevertheless remains.

There is one good thing about that climate. It reduces the risk of the kind of self-deception

Modern Idolatry

I alluded to just now, where for instance a sense of responsibility becomes an excuse for exploitation. In all other respects I believe it is bad. Responsibility is food for the will, guilt is food for the feelings only. It is one thing to accept responsibility for present wrongs and present sufferings resulting from old, unhappy far-off things and exploitings long ago, and to feel bound to try and set them right; it is another to feel guilty over them. Mistakenly guilty, for after all I am *not* personally accountable for wrongs perpetrated years before I was born, though I may choose to shoulder a personal responsibility for helping to set them right. I can think of two reasons in particular why it is bad. Such confused feelings of guilt tend to beget paralysis rather than energy. Those who are old enough to remember the years between the wars will recall the skillful use Hitler made of just that paralysis in the 30s, when even young people, who were in their cradles at the time it was signed, were somehow made to feel guilty about the unjust provisions of the Treaty of Versailles. The result was that the whole country looked helplessly on, instead of acting, while he armed and established his Germany a second time over for the conquest of the world.

There is another, and more deadly, reason. When they do not beget paralysis, feelings of guilt tend to turn rather easily into feelings of hatred and contempt. We may feel a bit guilty ourselves, but we are very sure that a whole lot of other people are much *more* guilty, and probably ought to be destroyed. This vindictiveness makes itself felt even through the sublime humility of the Psalmist. On the one hand: "As for me, I am a worm, and no man: a very scorn of men and the outcast of the people . . ." or "I acknowledge my faults: and my sin is ever before me." But on the other hand: "My heart sheweth me the wickedness of the ungodly: that there is no fear of God before his eyes. . . . The ungodly are froward, even from their mother's womb: as soon as they are born, they go astray and speak lies . . . let them consume away like a snail. . . . Break their teeth, O God, in their mouth. . . . Blessed shall be he that taketh [their] children: and throweth them against the stones . . ." and so on.

And just this darker side to the experience of guilt seems to be even more evident when

Modern Idolatry

the experience is collective than when it is individual. "All are responsible for all," said Alyosha in *The Brothers Karamazov*. A noble, a truly *human* sentiment — perhaps the only *absolutely* human sentiment there is. And how much less far we are from collectively realizing it than in the days, not so very long ago, when not only the blacks in America but "the servant class," or "the lower orders," or just "the poor," as they were called in England, were regarded almost as a different species, for whose welfare we were responsible, if at all, only to a very limited extent! That is surely well, and very well. It is the irritation of guilt that turns it into the impulse to compel, into a determination to use every kind of violence, every device of indoctrination, in order to enforce on all a systematic equality that must entail a mechanical and inhuman uniformity.

It is real enough, this feeling of collective sin; no less real than the soft-pedaling of individual sin. And clearly it originates in the unconscious; for it is there that we experience collectively rather than individually. Now it is a characteristic of the unconscious, as understood by modern psychology, not only that the soul, or, if you prefer it, the psyche is sick, but that it is sick for some reason of which it is unaware; and further that it attributes that sickness to all manner of causes except the true one. This reflection makes me an attentive listener when I am told that the true cause of our feeling of collective guilt is not any of the causes to which our surface consciousness is ready to assign it, but rather that very alienation to which I devoted the earlier part of this lecture.

It is also the reason why I feel that an understanding, or rather a perceptive realization, of the essentially figurative nature of language is important. Such a realization can take us back into a consciousness, which was *not* alienated, which was not cut off from its immaterial source. For when the immaterial is actually perceived along with the material, it is self-evidently real and there is no temptation to dismiss or forget it. The fact that our inmost selves are part of a wider, inner world is then as obvious as the fact that our physical bodies are part of a wider physical world. And the nature of language, largely fossilized now but

Modern Idolatry

once wholly figurative, points us back to such a time.

Some very clever people have never learned that it is possible not only to *use* language but also to contemplate it. The same is true of consciousness itself. If I can never see the back of my head by whisking myself round, I can nevertheless see it pretty clearly in a mirror; and language contemplated is a mirror of my consciousness and its evolution.

The antidote to wrongs done in the past is restitution. But the only antidote to *feelings* of guilt, whether individual or collective, is repentance. It is again Paul Ricoeur who reminds us that in the Old Testament there is no abstract word for repentance, only the symbol of "returning." And it is such a returning to the source from which we have cut ourselves off — or, in an older idiom, from which we have "fallen" — that I believe is needed. Not of course a literal returning to the past by way of H. G. Wells's time-machine, but a return by re-experiencing the past in the present. It is in the present that we live, and it is our present condition, the very isolation and detachment of our self-consciousness, that has for the first time rendered possible that contemplation of the past, and its re-enactment in imagination, that is called "history."

Without that, it is not only the world of our perceptions, the world of nature, from which each of us must grow more isolated, but also from each other. For it is in the deepest realm of the unconscious that men really *are* one. It is there we must look both for our source and our goal, and we can only approach nearer to our goal by remembering our source. If literalness is our collective sin, history is our collective memory. Or we can make it so. And if it is etymologically no more than a pun, it is nevertheless a profound truth, that it is only by remembering our source that we can hope to *"re-member"* our true selves in a truly human community, instead of building up all manner of defenses and strategies to defend our empty artificial selves by fortifying them in their isolation.

A patient, sensitive contemplation of language in its historical reality is one way into just such a remembering. I do not say it is the only way, but it is perhaps one that is espe-

Modern Idolatry

cially adapted to those whose primary concern is with the humanities. It is in that milieu that the word "literalness" can properly be used. Almost inevitably such a contemplation returns the mind to a position much nearer to its original source; and therefore to what can be perceived from that vantage point.

> Not in entire forgetfulness,
> And not in utter nakedness,
> But trailing clouds of glory do we come
> From God, who is our home.

Wordsworth was speaking of course of the individual child; but he might equally well have been speaking of the birth of humanity itself. Language becomes for us, not a tool invented by individual minds, but an echo reverberating from the source of all individual minds, of all individual selves.

"Clouds of glory": how romantic it sounds! How remote from the tone that is most insistent in the academic world we mostly know of or hear from today! How remote, let me say more specifically, from a guilt-ridden sociology erected on an empty behavioral psychology! I am left wondering what

Owen Barfield

chances there are of its being realized, before it is too late, that the rising tide of sickness which therapeutic psychology is more and more thoughtfully struggling to stem is correlative to the literalness on which academic psychology is so imperturbably established and which it is so industriously engaged in riveting on the minds of the rising generation.

3

The Force of Habit

THIS IS THE THIRD of the three lectures I have been so kindly invited to give in Vancouver. I believe the position is that some people are enjoying the high privilege of sitting through all three of them, while others are having to make do with two or even only one of the three. I don't often come to Vancouver — not because I don't want to, but because I happen to live about 6,000 miles away — and perhaps for that reason, when I came to prepare them, I couldn't help thinking of the whole venture as a single project, and of the three lectures, even though not all given in the same place, as in some sense forming a single whole. I hope that unity is nevertheless a tri-unity — I have tried to make it so — and that any single one of the lectures

Owen Barfield

has made, or will make some sense taken by itself. I shall be obliged, in this lecture, to refer at times to matters dealt with in the two preceding ones, but I will try, with the help of a little unashamed repetition, to do so clearly and fully enough to meet at least the minimum requirements of those who did not hear them.

One of the points I tried to make, at some length, in the first lecture, which concerned the evolution of consciousness, was this: that it is a mistake — though it is a mistake that we nearly all make all the time, and we all make nearly all the time — to imagine that inward and immaterial component of the totality we call "the world" as being a sort of something located and confined inside our heads. Perhaps I should pause here to acknowledge the existence of some who tell us they easily avoid that mistake, because they go one step further and deny that there is any such experience as consciousness — or indeed any such experience as experience. There is the brain, they say, and there is the rest of the world that is not the brain, and there is [a] causal relation between them. But I should be wasting your time by paying them further attention, since such a po-

sense requires "no".

The Force of Habit

sition is only open to people who are incapable of distinguishing between one idea and another quite different idea; in this case, between what is meant by "perceiving" (which is one idea) and what is meant by "being perceptible" (which is a totally other idea).

There is however another pair, the clear distinction between which can be lost sight of even by the intelligent. In this case they both lie *within* the realm of inner experience, or consciousness, and they are called respectively "perceiving" and "thinking." The distinction between the two is primary and fundamental — axiomatic, if you like — because at any moment we choose we can make it a matter of immediate experience. It is nevertheless a distinction which it is rather easy to lose sight of, once we begin to reflect or philosophize, for this reason: that the single experience we call "consciousness" — our inwardness at any moment — is not composed either of perceiving alone or of thinking alone, but of an immemorial and inextricable combination of the two. Indeed it is better to call it an interpenetration rather than a combination. We soon learn, once we begin to reflect, that

Owen Barfield

what we have been accustomed to refer to in everyday speech as "perceiving" — as for instance when we speak of perceiving a chair or a blackboard, or for that matter a neuron or a chromosome — is in fact perception heavily laced with thinking, with habitual thought, with mental habit. It is impossible to separate the one from the other. And I was concerned to emphasize, in that lecture, that the fact of our being unable to separate them (as for instance, we can actually separate the salt in the sea from the water in the sea) is no good reason for ceasing to distinguish clearly between them. On the contrary, for it is just when we maintain the distinction, while realizing the interpenetration, that we are forced to the conclusion, which I will quote from the same lecture, that "Consciousness is not a tiny bit of the world stuck on to the rest of it. It is the inside of the whole world; or, if we are using the term in its stricter sense — excluding therefore the subconscious mind — then it is *part* of the inside of the whole world."

I must apologize for this hurried run-through of the groundwork. If you are interested but not convinced, you can easily pur-

The Force of Habit

sue it for yourselves at leisure — and without going into phenomenology and all that — by reading, for instance, a little book called *The Sciences and the Humanities* by W. T. Jones,[1] or even the opening chapters of my own book *Saving the Appearances.* It was put a little differently by the writer of an article in the *Harvard Review:* "We can see that there really is no outside world and no inside world. There is just one world." The title of the article, to which I will return, is "Our 'Polar Partnership' with the World around Us."[2]

Now if you are, or if you become convinced, that what we perceive is inseparable from how we think, which is the same as saying that the world around us is inseparable from the way we think — though it is certainly not *indistinguishable* from it — then a lot of things follow. One of them is the privilege of discovering how very differently mankind as a whole used to think in the remote past. By that I do not mean simply that they did not for the most part think analytically, logically, causally. Many anthropologists and others have

1. Berkeley: University of California Press, 1967.
2. January–February 1978.

Owen Barfield

discovered that, without however making the discovery I am referring to. I mean that the thoughts themselves were images rather than concepts. And this entails that the world they lived in was different from the world we live in today. It would be as true, perhaps truer, to say that they *perceived* images as to say that they thought them. What we perceive as things they perceived as images, and it is this discovery which enables us to grasp the distinction between the history of ideas and the history of consciousness.

The difference between an image and a thing lies in the fact that an image presents itself as an exterior expressing or implying an interior, whereas a thing does not. When what begins by being an image becomes in course of time a mere thing, we are justified in describing it as an *idol*. And a collective state of mind, which perceives all things and no images, may thus fairly be characterized as idolatry. This, and some of its consequences, was what my second lecture was mainly concerned with. The world we perceive around us today is no longer a world of images, no longer therefore an exterior expressing an interior, but simply a

The Force of Habit

brittle exterior surface, which is however not the surface *of* anything. And this reflection leads us to yet another discovery we can make; namely, that the quality of the world we live in is determined not only by what we perceive but also by what we *fail* to perceive. At the same time, if we have not only started from that interpenetration of thinking and feeling, with which I began, but have been careful not to lose sight of it as we proceed, we shall realize — perhaps with something of a shock — that this world of outsides with no insides to them, which we perceive around us and in which we dwell, is not something unshakably and unalterably given, but is largely the product of the way we collectively and subconsciously think. It is correlative to our mental habit.

The real world, the *whole* world, does not consist only of the things *of* which we are conscious; it consists also of the consciousness and subconsciousness that are correlative to them. They are the immaterial component of the world. But today the only immaterial element our mental habit acknowledges is our own little spark of self-consciousness. That is why we feel detached, isolated, cut off not only from the world as it really is, but also from those other little sparks of detached self-consciousness we acknowledge in our fellow human beings.

It was this "cut-offness," this *imprisonment* — for that is what it really is — that I tried to speak further of in that lecture, when I suggested that much that we notice round us today can be traced to it. For instance, the growing prevalence of mental disease, and again the uneasy sense of guilt that has come to pervade our society and, still more perhaps, our sociology. How much of it is really prison-sickness? Of course not many people actually think of themselves as in prison. They only feel it. They feel it because virtually everything that is thought and written today, from science to literature and criticism, from sociology to aesthetics, from theology to politics and in politics from extreme right to extreme left, is thought and written within the walls of that prison.

I suppose the most important question for a prisoner is, whether or not there is any way of escaping; and that is the question I am really

The Force of Habit

most concerned with today. It sounds as if it ought to be easy enough, where the prison in question is not made of steel and concrete, but only of mental habit. But it is not. Remember it is not just my mental habit, or your mental habit. It is *our* mental habit. I can philosophize myself free from philosophical materialism quite easily; and so, I dare say, can you. But what we are now talking about is *collective* mental habit, which is a very different matter. For that means that, after we have done the philosophizing and gone back to ordinary life, the materialism is still there in our very instruments of thought, and indeed of perception: it signifies that it is there in the meanings of the words we speak and think with, and notably so in the commonest words of all — words like "thing," "life," "man," "fact," "think," "perceive," and so on. It is not merely a habit, but an ingrained habit. It is even what we call "common sense."

As long as we have done nothing to change this common sense, this subconscious foundation of our consciousness, we have not begun the business of escaping at all. All our theories are simply different ways of occupying ourselves in prison. Whereas what is really needed is to begin scraping a tunnel beneath its walls. And of course we shall never begin on that if we do not even feel the walls are there. The first step of all is to realize that mental habit *is* a prison. One way, probably the most effective way, in which that realization can be brought about is by recalling our own history, that is the history of mankind, as thinking and perceiving beings; by contemplating in fact the history of consciousness. And one way, again, of doing that — it may or may not be the best way, but it is a way to which I happen to have given particular attention — is by contemplating the history of words and their meanings. But one way or another, what matters is our coming to realize that the way we habitually think and perceive is not the only possible way, not even a way that has been going on very long. It is the way we have *come* to think, the way we have *come* to perceive.

Habit is the end product of repeated action in the past, of prolonged behavior in the past. That is as true of mental habit as of any other. And so, if men have at last become incapable of seeing what they once saw, it is because they

The Force of Habit

have gone on for a long time not looking at it. To realize that fact is, as I say, the necessary first step; but it is only the first step and does not take us very far. It is the odd bit of iron we have found lying about in the prison, and with which we can now begin scraping. But the scraping itself? How *does* one break oneself of a habit — especially if it is an ingrained one? It is not so easy. Just willing yourself to get rid of it by behaving differently will not work. The only effective way is deliberately to form a new habit at variance with the old one. That also is very difficult, but not impossible. When you were young, you probably learned to ride a bicycle. It was difficult at first, and you kept falling off. But in the end your repeated actions during the learning stage died, or rather lived, into an ingrained habit of balancing on two wheels. It may have been a bit difficult to form that habit, but it was not nearly so difficult as it would be now to get rid of it; to "outgrain" the ingrained habit and return yourself to the condition you were in the first time you mounted, when, instead of automatically turning the handlebars a trifle in the direction to which the machine was leaning, you turned them the other way and fell off. Try learning *not* to ride a bicycle! Once you are on the saddle, you will find your muscles just won't obey you. They will obey your habit instead. You will find you simply *can't* turn the wheel in the wrong direction, so as to fall off. You discover that habit has a will of its own, a sort of frozen, unconscious will that is much stronger than the little bit of will you are consciously exerting. It is as if you were trying to ignore a law of nature.

What sort of new habit, then, should we try to form in order to get rid of the ingrained mental habit I have been speaking of? I believe it must be the habit of thinking *actively;* of choosing to think, instead of letting our thoughts just happen. You have to begin, as with forming any other habit, by performing, or trying to perform, the same action repeatedly; from time to time, and for short periods, doing nothing else except choosing what you will think about, and (perhaps even more important) what you will *not* think about, as long as the period lasts. It doesn't much matter whether you dignify what you are doing by the name of "meditation" or not. At

The Force of Habit

all events there are other practices going by
that name (often no doubt quite justifiably)
which have little to do with what I am referring to. It is not so impossibly difficult, this
preliminary effort. It may be a long time before
thinking actively turns into anything like a
habit, but other things will begin to happen
long before that. For instance, almost at the
outset, you will encounter head-on what Coleridge called, in a pregnant phrase, "the mind's
self-experience in the act of thinking."[3] And
simply out of that encounter you are likely to
make all sorts of incidental discoveries. Here is
one of them.

You may have noticed that nearly at the
beginning I spoke of something that can be lost
sight of "even by the intelligent." In conjunc-
tion with what went before there was a somewhat snide suggestion there that materialists,
or reductionists, or behaviorists — call them
what you will — are not intelligent, because
they overlook the obvious. This was unfair; in
fact it was the product of irritation, rather than
sober reflection. Many of that ilk are very in-

3. *Biographia Literaria,* chapter XII.

telligent indeed, and certainly so, if what we
have in mind by "intelligence" is mental agil-
ity. It is just that what is obvious to others is
not obvious to them. Well, you now discover
that the theory that consciousness, or personality, or self — again, call it what you will — is
merely a fiction, ought not to be judged as a
theory at all; since, at bottom, it is not a conclusion of the judgment but an inclination of
the will. What is obvious to me, you say to
yourself, is not obvious to him at all, though it
could become so if he chose. We can always
choose not to look at what stares us in the face.
There is music, and we are not bound to listen
to it; there are colors, and we can turn away
from them; there are perfumes, and we can
choose to hold our noses; in the same way
there is a self, a wholly human and inner self
within each one of us, from which we are free,
if we prefer, to withhold our attention. There
is more than one version of the old story of the
man who languished for decades in prison
without ever trying the door, to see if it was
locked. When at last he did try it, he found it
had been unlocked all the time. Perhaps, if
Coleridge had lived today, when the rot has

The Force of Habit

gone so much deeper than in his day, he would have spoken not of self-experience, but of self-discovery in the act of thinking.

Another result is this. The fact that, by contrast with perceiving, thinking comes from within; the fact that, by contrast with perceiving, it is something we *do,* and not merely something that happens to us, is now, for us, a matter of immediate experience. Accordingly, we cease to be bemused by that failure to distinguish thinking from perceiving of which I spoke earlier in this lecture, and at greater length in the first of these three lectures. Hitherto the trouble was that we only knew it as a very feeble and inert kind of doing, a very supine kind of activity. Now we have discovered that we can, if we choose, make it otherwise and, once that has happened, we are no longer in danger of losing sight of the distinction.

Another consequence, and a more important one: your thinking will begin to put on the muscle of imagination; or if that is already there, to strengthen it. It was again Coleridge who divined the relation between imagination and will, and demonstrated it through the careful distinction he made between imagination on the one hand and fancy, which is passive, on the other. Imagination is really thinking with a bit of will in it. You may be supposing I mean by this that you will now start writing good poetry. That is not what I mean at all, though it is one possible side effect. Imagination is not the fenced preserve of poetry, or even of the fine arts in general; and no one saw that more clearly than George Eliot, when she remarked, in *Daniel Deronda:* "Here undoubtedly lies the chief poetic energy: — in the force of imagination that pierces or exalts the solid fact, instead of floating among cloud-pictures."

As you know, my real topic is *collective* habit. If I have spent some time on individual mental habit, and the breaking of it, it is because in the end a collective habit can be broken down into a large number of individual ones — and it is only an individual who can begin to break them, thereby making his minute contribution to the breaking of the collective habit. Everything has to begin somewhere. Let me quote once more, as follows, from that

The Force of Habit

impressive article in the *Harvard Review* to which I have already referred you.

> It is not error in grand policies that endangers our planet, but imprisonment in our own minds, which, if set free, would guide us individually first of all and collectively after all.

To which the author, Professor Edwin H. Land, adds this further observation:

> The first step in freeing the mind of its own chains is to turn it towards reverence, insight, and appreciation of itself.

Generally speaking, metaphors are more illuminating, if we do not confine ourselves too tightly to a single one. One can think of a hole made in a prison wall — but one can also think of what happens after a hole — quite a small one — has been made in a sea wall or a dyke.

One of the consequences that must follow, I believe, as the *collective* habit begins to crumble, is a consequence for natural science. Once the muscle of imagination begins to make itself felt *there,* its thinking, and therewith its methodology, must begin adapting themselves to the investigation of other laws of nature, in addition to the class to which they are at present confined, namely the principle of causality and the so-called "laws" of chance or randomness. No doubt the world can be thought as a sequence of causes and effects; but it can also be thought as a sequence of patterns, of forms changing into other forms. One can go further than that. Can the *life* in nature really be adequately thought in any other way? By treating it exclusively as a sequence of causes and effects, are we not in effect struggling to grasp the whole of nature with an imprisoned thinking that is in truth only applicable to the inanimate part of it? It was a firm conviction to that effect that made Goethe, at the end of his life, attach more importance to his scientific than to his literary output.

I have had to mention science, because science (I mean the causality-science which is all we yet have) is clearly the most impenetrable one of the prison walls we call "common sense." Indeed for the man of today common sense consists largely of what he has been told

The Force of Habit

by science, either directly or by the way in which other subjects have been presented to him in the course of his education. How much of *that* is traceable to habit rather than to open-minded enquiry? Alas, I cannot deal with everything. But read, if you have not done so already, T. S. Kuhn's book *The Structure of Scientific Revolutions*.[4] In any case such a change of atmosphere in the scientific establishment is only relevant, in the long view I have been taking, as one of the prerequisites to a change in common sense.

You may have noticed that that *Harvard Review* article did not speak of imprisonment in our own minds as endangering *us*, it spoke of endangering "our planet." Why? We are brought back once more to the cardinal reflection that consciousness is not just the inside of us; it is the inside of the world. And you do not change the inside of a living organism without at the same time changing the outside. Thomas Kuhn had realized this, when he spoke in the book I have referred to, of transformations of the "imagination in ways that we shall ulti-

4. Chicago: University of Chicago Press, 1962.

mately need to describe as a transformation of the world."

Perhaps you are pulling yourselves up sharp by now. Very interesting, but he is letting the subject run away with him. Very impressive, this notion that by changing ourselves we change the world we live in. But it just won't wash. When all's said and done, nature is something that goes on by itself. We can change ourselves, develop our imaginations, and all that caper, till we are blue in the face, and it will go on going on just the same. If I jump off the roof of a house, I shall still fall and break my neck, whatever I and the rest of humanity have been collectively thinking and perceiving. Nature's behavior does not depend on human consciousness, it depends on the laws of nature. That's just common sense; and it's time we got back to it!

If anyone should be reacting in that way, I would ask him to pause with me for a moment to reflect on that useful phrase "the laws of nature." People talk of them in a familiar and confident way, but how many ever stop and ask themselves what they really mean by it?

The Force of Habit

Try doing just that! Try quoting Shakespeare at them. Ask them:

> What is your substance, whereof are you made?

Oh well, you say, they are just a part of nature. But *are* they? Do we really even think they are? The one thing, above all, that we know about nature is that it has been, from the beginning of time or as far back as we can peer, in a constant process of evolution, of *change*. How is it then that this particular bit of it that we call the laws of nature has *never* changed? Or so we are told. How is it that we are as certain of that (for the whole current idea of evolution is based on just that assumption)[5] as we are that the rest of nature has gone on changing all the time? One would have expected those — and their number is legion — who are convinced that *everything* is accounted for by biology, to perceive that difficulty. But some-

---

5. When this assumption first began to be made, it was called the "uniformitarian" *hypothesis*. But the fact of its being a hypothesis, and necessarily an unproven one, has long been conveniently lost sight of.

how they don't. Perhaps because to give up assuming immutable laws of nature would mean giving up that neatly simplified model of evolution called the Darwinian theory.[6]

Well then, if the laws it is governed by are not part of biological nature, what are they? Where are we to look for them? In the mind of course, comes the answer. Did not Immanuel Kant say something of the sort? He certainly did; but what is generally overlooked, or forgotten, or slurred over, is the enormous difference between the one way of looking at them and the other. Perhaps it is partly because Kant himself rather overlooked that, that even those — and again their name is legion — who are convinced that the so-called "laws of nature" are part of the mind, are content to go on treating them as though they were part of nature.

You will have seen by now the direction in

6. It is still as neat as a new suit of clothes in the popular mind and — as in Freud's day — almost everywhere else outside of professionally zoological circles, where it now appears to be conspicuous mainly by its large holes and the queer patches over them. See also chapter 2, note 5, above.

The Force of Habit

which this part of my argument is pointing. If there should be time for questions afterwards, I can foresee someone getting up and asking me bluntly: "Are you seriously saying that the laws of nature are simply mental habits?" I rather hope he won't, because there are considerations going beyond the scope of this lecture which make it impossible to answer such a question with a naked yes or no. It would raise once more the question I mentioned and declined to answer at the end of my first lecture: whether evolution proper ended when history began, or whether it is continuing alongside of it. Moreover, if one is rash enough to peer into the future at all, it makes a big difference whether he is taking a short view or a medium-length view or a very, very long one. Let me instead put the question in rather a different way, but one that is closely allied to it. When one speaks of the "force of habit," is he using the word "force" wholly as a metaphor? Is the force we are alluding to categorically different from the forces of nature, as we call them, or is there a generic link between them? Instead of giving my own answer to that question I will try, in conclusion, to leave you with some reflections that may have a bearing on the way in which, either now or later on, you answer it for yourselves.

In the course of that lecture it became necessary to point out that it is the nature of thought to be universal. It is the element of thought in our perception of a chair that magically fuses it with all other chairs, present or absent, actual or possible, and so enables us to give it a *name*. But, paradoxically, it is equally the nature of thought to be particular; for it was also the element of thought in our perceiving that enabled us in the first place to isolate that chair from the whole perceptual surround, to identify it, to be aware that this is this object and no other. It was this *also,* then, that enabled us to name it. It is the name, the word, that particularizes; and it does so because it generalizes, and *by* generalizing. It is in this paradoxical quality of conceptualization — one in all, but appropriated by each — that the possibility of what we call "meaning" resides.

But if it is the nature of thought to be at the same time both particular and universal, there is something else also, whose nature is turning

The Force of Habit

out to be much the same. I mean the something
that is investigated, not by philosophers, but
by physicists. They have been investigating it
for a long time, concentrating their efforts on
isolating or identifying the smallest bit of it
there is, formerly called the atom, but since the
advent of the nuclear age by some such name
as the ultimate particle. I will go on calling it
the atom, for short. And the two most recent
things to have been discovered, or at any rate
believed, about the atom are these. First, that it
is not a particle at all, in the sense understood
by the earlier physicists, that is, a tiny bit of
what common sense calls "matter," which is
something like a speck of dust, but something
more like the point of intersection of energies
or forces. And the second is that it has to be
conceived as present not only at the point
in space where it has been identified, but
everywhere throughout the world.

It is a little more than 130 years since
Michael Faraday suggested (to quote his actual
words) that

> matter is not merely mutually penetrable, but
> each atom extends, so to say, throughout the

whole of the solar system, yet retaining its own centre of force.[7]

Being a cautious and conscientious scientist, he put it forward as a suggestion only; but I think you will find it is a view which has been gaining ground fairly steadily since his time.

The reflection I should like to leave you with — or perhaps it should rather be called another question — is this. Is this resemblance between the nature of thought, as we know it to be, and the nature of matter, as it has begun to be conceived to be — at once particular and universal — merely a curious coincidence, or should we conclude from it that thought and the atom consist of one and the same substance? (I use the word "substance," because there is no other; it can be objected to only if the question it raises has been begged in advance.) I greatly fear that that question is no longer a merely academic one. And for this reason: that we live in an age when precisely the second conclusion is beginning to be ar-

7. *Experimental Researches in Electricity*, London, 1844.

The Force of Habit

rived at — and from the wrong direction. Not
from within the humanities, where the true
motivation is the advance of knowledge, and
of the wisdom into which it may turn; but
from other quarters, where the sole motivation
is the advance of technology and of the power
over others that technology can confer. Indica-
tions of this, some less and some more subtle,
are there for those who are awake to the
signs of the times. Some of you, for instance,
probably saw Sheila Ostrander and Lynn
Schroeder's book *Psychic Discoveries behind
the Iron Curtain,*[8] which came out in 1970,
and perhaps you took the trouble to sift its
factual content from the garb of sensational
journalese in which it is presented. If so, you
must have sensed, as I did, a sinister combination of physical research not only with experimental physiology, but also with experimental
psychology and parapsychology. Such a concept as that of "psychotrons" is born in minds
that are interested, not in changing or redeem-
ing the force of their own mental habit, but in
manipulating that of others. And this kind of

8. Prentice-Hall.

research is now being financed by governments.

Some say that evolution has now reached a stage at which man himself is becoming increasingly responsible for it. As you will have gathered, I think the same; but I do not see that responsibility at all as others see it. George Steiner once coined a useful phrase when he referred to our contemporary habit of "biologizing the data," and these people all seem to think only in terms of an evolution biologically determined, and therefore of the application of technology to the data, whether by genetic engineering or otherwise. Whereas I am certain that our responsibility will only be discharged, if at all, not by tinkering with the outside of the world but by changing it, slowly enough no doubt, from the inside.

These, then, are the kinds of reasons why I am anxious that, as time goes on, the humanities departments in universities here and elsewhere should come to interest themselves in these matters a good deal more than they have hitherto done. It would be good if even a Department of English, in addition to the more detailed and sharply focused aspects

The Force of Habit

of its discipline which it rightly pursues —
such as the influence, if any, of Henry James on
Marcel Proust — should occasionally extend
its gaze towards the rather far-reaching considerations which your generous hospitality
and your patient attention have encouraged
me to try and open up in these lectures.

A Note

THE THREE CHAPTERS of this book reproduce with a few slight alterations and additions three lectures given before audiences in Vancouver during October 1978, two of them at the University of British Columbia and one at the Vancouver Institute. The order in which they appear is the order in which they were intended to be delivered, though for a reason which has no bearing on their content it became necessary to reverse the order of 1 and 2.

I fear a bibliography is out of the question, since it would include a fair proportion of all the books, both ancient and modern, I have ever read or looked into, including not a few expressing views very different from my own. In addition to those referred to in the text however it may be worthwhile to mention a few others which have come my way, and which are perhaps more definitely relevant than the general run to the topic of these lectures. They include:

Owen Barfield

Erich Auerbach. *Scenes from the Drama of European Literature: Six Essays* (notably the long opening chapter headed "Figura"). Magnolia, Massachusetts: Peter Smith, 1973.

Nicolas Berdyaev. *The Meaning of History*. London: G. Bles, 1949. New York: C. Scribner's, 1936.

J. H. van den Berg. *The Changing Nature of Man*. New York: Dell Publishing, 1961.

Ernst Cassirer. *Language and Myth*. Translated by Susanne K. Langer. New York: Dover Publications, 1946.

——— . *The Philosophy of Symbolic Forms*, Vol. 1: *Language*. Translated by Ralph Manheim. New Haven: Yale University Press, 1953; and other books.

Francis Cornford. *From Religion to Philosophy: A Study in the Origins of Western Speculation*. London: 1912. Magnolia, Massachusetts: Peter Smith, 1958.

Mircea Éliade. *Images et Symboles*. Mission, Kansas: Sheed Andrews & McMeel, Inc., 1969; and other books.

René Guénon. *Reign of Quantity*. Metaphysical Library Series. New York: Penguin Books, 1972; and other books.

Erich Neumann. *Origin and History of Consciousness*. Translated by R. F. Hull. Bollingen

A Note

Series, Vol. 42. Princeton, New Jersey: Princeton University Press, 1970.

Richard B. Onians. *The Origin of European Thought About the Body, the Mind, the Soul, the World, Time, and Fate.* The Philosophy of Plato and Aristotle Series. New York: Arno Press, Inc., 1951.

Elizabeth Sewell. *Orphic Voice: Poetry and Natural History.* New York: Harper & Row, 1971.

Bruno Snell. *Discovery of the Mind: The Greek Origins of European Thought.* New York: Harper & Row, 1960.

Pierre Teilhard de Chardin. *Phenomenon of Man.* New York: Harper & Row, 1959.

In all of the above, and no doubt in a number of others which unfortunately do not now come to mind, I seem to myself to have detected a move, or a speculative tendency to move on from history of ideas and into evolution of consciousness. I must add what I have already made clear in most of my own books (whereof a list of those in print will be found at the beginning of this book), that for a full treatment of the subject, both extensive and intensive, clearly based on actual *knowledge* of it, I have found nowhere to go outside the works of Rudolf Steiner.